AMERICAN FAITH

MAYA C. POPA

Louisville, KY
2019

AMERICAN
FAITH

SARABANDE BOOKS

Library of Congress Cataloging-in-Publication Data
Names: Popa, Maya C., 1989– author.
Title: American faith : poems / Maya C. Popa.
Description: First edition. | Louisville, KY : Sarabande Books, 2019.
Identifiers: LCCN 2019010490 (print) | LCCN 2019013530 (e-book)
ISBN 9781946448477 | ISBN 9781946448460 (acid-free paper)
Classification: LCC PS3616.O6484 (e-book) | LCC PS3616.O6484 A6 2019 (print)
DDC 811/.6—dc23
LC record available at https://lccn.loc.gov/2019010490

Cover and interior design by Alban Fischer
Cover image: "Split" (2013) by Ben Zank
Manufactured in Canada.
This book is printed on acid-free paper.
Sarabande Books is a nonprofit literary organization.

This project is supported in part by an award from the National Endowment for the Arts.
The Kentucky Arts Council, the state arts agency, supports Sarabande Books with
state tax dollars and federal funding from the National Endowment for the Arts.

For my parents, who gave us America, and me, everything

And for Sam

CONTENTS

AMERICAN FAITH

MINE'S NOT A POLITICAL HEART

All of my childhood fantasies—icescapes
with Alaskan cranes, treasure diving
in the Black Sea—Putin has beat me to them.

He drapes a medal over his shadow
then extradites the dead from purgatory.
I live with this deadweight of humor

and scorn until the humor burns out.
I know my birthmarks aren't heraldic,
the sunspots transcribed don't form

a line of sheet music. Blinking, I kill
a group of gnats; *I kill only to see clearly.*
Give me refuge from that sentence,

freedom from the choir sanctioning.
Each day, the grail looks more like a chalice.
Each day, the chalice more like a mug.

THE GOVERNMENT HAS BEEN CANCELED

and my friend has just dissected a body in medical school,
of which we have not spoken, knowing there are privacies

we must pretend are still intact.   The panda cam is off: people
                                                   are distressed

that someone will forget to feed the cub
unless the live feed's breathing in the toolbar. I spend the afternoon

dreaming a rebellion I could stage
                              and still show up to my body the next morning,

            life the way it was promised
on sitcoms where everyone gets to be alive for twenty minutes
        not worrying about the debt ceiling or health insurance.

My friend makes the first of many incisions
into that cold, familiar otherness.

I turn to obituaries for proof
that people still matter to one another
        in towns where stores bear the names of the deceased.

            Today, the Library of Congress is canceled

which makes it difficult to do my job,

checking dates of publications and answering questions

such as *are preachers and reverends interchangeable in most faiths.*

From this description, it is impossible to say what I do.

I go home burdened and amplified by knowledge,

live in the world this information refers to—

there is no better, other way to do this.

The government is canceled

but not the body: not the bodies furloughed

not the bodies waiting

for my friend to break them tenderly.

SINAIA, ROMANIA

Corridors of calves   cataract of mountains
lands pulled up by the navel   then abandoned
they say   by a dry god   on the occasion of a drink.

These, the Carpathians my father saw each morning
not seeing the film of forest from the sky.

He played the same trick for six years,
dressed the classroom skeleton in old clothes
so the teacher would tousle his hair.

Some things you never punish.
Some superstitions turn their backs to god:

>*keep a pelt on the roof to thwart*
>*the falling stars,*

>*your mother's hair*
>*so she won't bury you first.*

In Sinaia, my grandfather kept wild dogs
in case a man tried to steal one of his daughters.

Watered by barks, the wrong crops grew.
The hen's eggs turned a vicious red.

Some things a god will punish twice.

Now, not a single steward stays,
not even for American dollars.

That there are things we will not let money buy us
is a trick the stomach plays
staying full on water.

A god folding his couch the night he made
the Atlantic   a glass tossed
between rough stones.

THE MASTER'S PIECES

Iron violet, slingshot carnation, who doesn't envy the painter's do-overs,
doesn't dream of white's division, colors spun into a stupor.

The more I write, the leaner the binary. Two colors, one ascent
over twenty-six stepladders.

Who doesn't envy the painter's process, bodies kneaded out of light
into cool, uninjured nothingness.

A painter knows her subject when she sees it, figure all flood,
all inside-out wolf, as immediate a hook as any hitch in logic.

Writing seems absurd by comparison. My hands listen to my brain listens
to my listening. Black on flagstone, bodiless cursive

I write out and back in, and if I'm a master at anything, it's taking out
the names until something

reveals itself. The pleasure of a landscape is immediate:
there forever and by addition you all of a sudden; suddenly there's you

by the haystacks holding a bridle. Or is that the writer again
fawning on a feeling, dreaming of wool's division into further wool,

hoping to halve and to have and examine closely,
too closely, and still, to keep on having.

Every poem has something trying to escape
by a tear the length of its idiom. A name that can be vanquished

by anaphora. (Who doesn't envy that?) Then suddenly there's a *you* again
as per our lore. As per our lore, the sky tries to tell me something.

I look till there's no distance between me and the looking.

URANIUM IN ENGLISH

I.

A nuclear death shares
its colors with the parrotfish—

chainslick, moccasin,
icebreaker, gigawatt.

The Alabama Shot
stocks "My First Rifles,"

guns in a variety of colors,
pink for girls to shoot squirrels.

I'm arranging information
available to anyone.

2.

I teach my class
the problem/solution structure.

Many logical questions are asked,
several logical solutions proposed.

What about the squirrels?
I ask my students.

Whole neighborhoods
annihilated in Hiroshima,

classrooms like cartoon
shadows in Nagasaki.

We agree one violence
is greater than the others,

but a string of tiny violences
makes the largest possible.

3.

A boy with a Crickett rifle
kills his sister in Kentucky.

No teacher can show him
how to live with it,

no diagram of the body,
no pull-down map

can illustrate the wound
spread across his days.

Not Latin odes, not physics—
his parents can't teach him,

nor the man who sold
his father this miniature

with the knowledge
he'd outgrow it

like a pair of shoes.

4.

In 1789, uranium is found
asleep aside anonymous metals.

The bullet, one could say,
was always inside of us,

the club a casual
extension of our arms.

And if all of our limitations
are armed, what's left

to keep a citizen clean,
what glove can fit

our knuckle's trigger?

5.

And don't imagine
it gets easier hearing about it,

I tell my students, or do I,
when they mention

another errant shooting,
nuclear test. And I worry

for the seasons which cannot
worry for each other,

summer like a fog that won't
dissolve, the end of snow.

Too late to worry, says Jorie—
I do not tell them this.

Instead, I ask, what color
is a disagreement between

friends, between nations—
what does being right look like?

And the shame is that the parrotfish
cannot be remade from scratch,

while the delicate,
collectible uranium glass

will glow into infinity,
a Vaseline sheen.

IS THIS YOUR BAG PLEASE WOULD YOU OPEN IT

The moment you know they are about to find something
pushing aside the mini marmalades
withdrawing the curler with latex fingers
folding a flap   folding back   another flap
your underwear grinning   not getting the situation
placed inside a box   PROPERTY OF HEATHROW
it isn't personal   though it sure feels
like it's personal   when a man asks you
how long you spent in Romania   when moments ago
you said you were in London   and packed your own
bag   who else would pack your fucking bag

but he thinks it's charming
to get things wrong   or maybe professional
to run on a hunch   he swipes the straps
for a bomb test   banters while your bras
feel badly for you   they never wanted this   in spite
of their lace   finally he finds the toiletries case   delays
the pleasure of admonishing you   for Alice-sized lotions
stolen from hotels   into another box they go
it's a job   remember   you can't take it personally
                    if he hands you his number on a food court receipt
                    prettiest terrorist I've seen all day
is this your privacy   and can he . . .

MY GODFATHER VOTES TRUMP

At twelve, he teaches me to dress like a girl, my brother to drink
and swear in Romanian. Harmless in that way that awaits practice,

eludes danger when the light's unhurried and long. He tends
a mutiny of white hydrangeas with dexterity disguised as care.

Names failures like flowers, which culture's laziest, what color
can't learn anything at all. In his study of injuries, intrinsic

shortcomings, strangers always abandoned their own,
letting sons get fat, join gangs, rape, languishing in payouts

drawn from his paycheck. Regretfully, we looked out the window
at the world. Nothing he taught us stuck. He blamed our mother,

loved women until they became people, human in some repellent way.
It was like watching bitters made, the root grown strange,

poisoned in its own perception. Still, he suffered his conviction
he was cheated, while better days awaited, preserved in the past,

layers of ice to some murky bottom. No one knows what will hold.
The hydrangeas take on color, copper. The season turns over

with perfect indifference. And I am twelve again, November, under
duress by a language, its failure to imagine the present world or next,

a recklessness my godfather seems to have authored. A darkness
that has always existed at the edges, demanding a license for the night.

YARD SALE

Books, aromatherapy kits, and sheet music—
objects that have lived in the presence of people
and will need new owners to remain relevant.
The cups would like to be adopted as a set,
the spaghetti measurer is skittish around children.
Someone has left a newspaper balancing
between two levels of a tiered table. The front page
glitters with bad news; anything good
is tucked into metaphor: a rollercoaster of
emotions later, the dog returns unharmed
and the family resumes its battles against
the perils on page 1. No one wants to buy anything.
They want to peer into each other's lives,
press their mouths to strangers' cups
and lift affinities, a few words of Swedish,
a talent for sudoku. I lay the news by the music
and patchouli to see if that will unbully it.
Someone organizes hurt by color, the blue table
dark as the underbelly of an avalanche.
There I place an orange napkin, copy of Keats,
and hope for a handover of idle goodness,
a share of warmth stored in our sugars
passed through the vellum of our touch.
Home, an ant drowns in my espresso.
I hold a vigil; I can still hear the voice of my teacher

reading the part of the ant in a picture book.
We're counted on to make a safety of our minds,
a world out of objects shared between us.
I kiss the cup held by my two hands.
My mouth might mend a stranger's mouth.

THE LYRIC I

Let the things that I'm afraid of
be things,

                let me see them through the lens
                of a woman's camera.

Winter snaps its tripod into place.

    The long-tailed jaeger, horned lark
    abdicate their thrones.

                I feed on what desire grows
                in its own gardens,

pines by the dozens,
the shape of you beyond them.

I move   a theft   between acres
                              of my selves,

while in the most unfashionable
of all possible presents,

                someone's Laura
                struggles with a shoelace.

She is not the roundabout
the moon inhabits.

Should I self-reduce
        to a shard in a hoof,

                who will hold me that close?

THE BEES HAVE BEEN CANCELED

Never again the humming, saddled flowers. Never the blind oath by a velveteen prisoner. Never the yellow, hula-hooped in black, little engine left running late into the darkness. Oh, how they were charming, clever monographs. Sunlight couldn't save them from the angel of extinction. Virgil said they swell with nectar's tilted knowledge. I don't know what to believe. Maybe they tired of being addicts. Clover honey, garbage honey, accidental ice cream honey. Ransomed stamen, sweetsinful will-do-anything-for honey. Maybe they caught fevers at midnight with no one there to hold their stingers, no fat queen to press a cold compress. How will we currency honey from wildflowers, that liquid of languages? How pollinate in the bees' electrostatic absence? How will the bellbirds take it, the Canterbury birds? Who will cast the last skeleton in amber? I'll miss the noise, the palimpsestic clamor, soft shock of discovering a hive under your roof. The lull as each integer walked its body over a blossom, then flew away with its instructions.

ELEGY

M. C., 1988–2003

I.

Lunch today is self-serve: cantaloupe and cold cuts,
candy corn from last October's open house,
still chews. Jam is a megachurch for wasps.

I swat, leave stingers in each purple sandwich.
The kids with allergies won't approach
the food station, fidget with EpiPens hidden

in their pockets. Humming near a blond boy's
perfect ear—it's the kind of joke I want to play,
dethroning his steeliness while I suck my own

stung tongue. I am thirteen. I take everything
personally. Hark the lost angels with irreverent
song lyrics. My friends and I weave box stitched key rings

our fathers will lose outside Hackensack homes.
Windfall hours, huddle under canopies,
curl our fists around foosball sticks and shove.

Love is missing a shot for someone cute.
The moon transfigures, distinguishes
our limits. West of here, September waits.

2.

I volunteer to dissect owl pellets
in nature class. How I'm not disgusted

confounds me. I have a chart
to tell apart the bones of mice,

ball and socket, vertebra and lower jaw,
each talismanic fragment the work

of a single meal. It was the promise
of identification I valued, an unconsumed

fixation on the known. That summer,
Matthew asked me out. He asked out

all the girls in our bunk, and like the others,
I said no in a voice borrowed from TV.

But suppose I'd been older and the boy
needed me. Suppose I'd bloomed early

into feminine kindness, could have mothered
him the way no one knew he needed.

3.

The afternoon the camp director tells us the news,

I'm waiting for a cue on the "adult reaction"

but devise it on my own, crying within sight

of a crush to invite his comfort.

At night I go home and look up the news—

Boy, 14. Dead. Abuse. I paint Matthew

as an angel and yell at my father

for reasons that confuse us both. A new world,

I don't say, not knowing what I mean,

what it will mean to me years from then.

No easy elegy for the one you didn't,

all things considered, work to befriend,

but one of yours regardless.

Dead from blunt force. His own mother.

No logic, no language will bring the boy back.

4.

On Friday, we plant a tree by the flagpole,
Hackensack frankincense,
rue for the drive-through.

The phrase *due process* looms
over our adulthood, a tree
whose branches bow to our reach.

The case is settled in 2009,
his mother sentenced
to three years.

He didn't even get to imagine
the confusion and assault
of all the other kinds of suffering,

having known only the one
that ends the pleasure of the others.

5.

Matthew, some camp news for you:
the cool boy I liked was bit by a cobra
he was keeping as a pet—can you believe it?

When I read that on the local news,
I thought, I'm better off not having had
that first kiss. Or is that joke a miss?

I mean, it's true, but does all pain
now seem a waste to you? I didn't write
when I knew you, thirteen, superficial

as a paper scratch. There's a you I carry
but can't reignite, that's still ·
a little me at thirteen, convinced,

unfinished, the world layering for later.
I hope you have a baseball mitt in heaven,
your favorite everything you had the time

to favor. I'm sorry I can't tell you
the Yankees score. I'm sorry for the hole
in the center of camp I've never been

back to. Accept the friendship I didn't
offer then, the care I would have shown
had I known how. I've read a bee

will buzz around a sleeping child for luck.
You will always be a child, asleep.
I'll always keep the latest news for you.

That summer lost its baby teeth
until the sun couldn't chew our skin
into a tan, and we retreated to our homes

like pale, astonished fish, and our friendships
bewildered us, coagulating, vanishing.

LEWISBURG

Longing, we say, because desire is full / of endless distances.

—Robert Hass

Driving down a highway in August, saving for later
the right word for now,   desire whittled me
a tool I'd never seen before
          but knew how to use almost immediately.

Tornadoes yellowed, revised the river & bovine lands
for sale beside it.

Longing, I said, pushing distance
through a cage—
it's why the picture city must be snowed in.

The other words I couldn't think of at the time,
like many things that leave before
          you've found a name for them.

SCALA NATURAE

Aristotle organized the living world into animals and plants. That was
    the easy part.

What separates us from animals is that we think about thinking, I tell
    my students
as we read the dystopias of their fathers' fathers, though they are mostly
    unimpressed with unattractive people killing one another for
    the state.

        Something delicate has been lifted from them,
        a fear we could slip from our own grasp.

Always a girl raises her hand to amend: *As far as we know, we are the only,*

extending the privilege, though it serves so little if the conclusion
    arrived at,
the thought thought through, lets the driver plow the sidewalk in
    an SUV,
bans the hungry crossing borders.

        Something like a sickness of the unfamiliar,
        the way we shiver at each other's names.

Occasionally, a predator spares the weaker species out of something,
    presumably,

not thinking about thinking. And I protect these exceptions with
amateur devotion, courage for an order that concedes to the weak,

that looks and really *sees*, and pities.

ON THE FORCES OF IMPROVISATION
UNDER THE GUN LAW

The first principle of improvisation is to say *yes*
no matter the line cast by your partner.
All must agree on the reality before them.

Yes, say the NRA, the Republican senators.

Improvisation is a game Samaritans play
as they run out of a movie theater,
serve as human shields for children.

Here, improvisation is also called humanity.

The principle of the gun law is that anyone
should have the right to buy what may kill
a room full of people—this failure is freedom.

I'm sorry there can't be more poetry in this.

A gun backer argues with the irreverence and zeal
of one who can never be proven wrong.

                              He is improvising.

He's of those men who depend
on my politeness, says to visualize which end
of the barrel you'd like to be on.

He owns a gun farm in Florida—
they grow in swamps like water chestnuts.

Watercolorists paint them year-round,
open barrels gleaming from the marshes.

MEDITATION HAVING FELT AND FORGOTTEN

after Robert Hass

All the new thinking is about preempting feeling.
In this way, it is incompatible with all the old thinking
but easier to stomach.
How birds land on water without closing their eyes
reminds me how I sought you with an appetite
more pressing than fear. And the year our passion took—
how flat to call it lust, how wrong to call its mimicry love
when little love was made with which to mistake it.

All the new thinking is about straightening the facts.
Your hands disappeared, water drying over weeks.
I learned that pain's the lack of place to point to.
Would have made the trade: me for you, us for anything.
Would have said anything over and over, *blackberry*,
dance party, *silverfish* like Typhon imitating voices.
What an unfair tax on time desire is,
a year of spell work to break that staring contest.

All the new thinking is about drugging up
to let go of the mark desire leaves on the body.
The new thinking's about saying goodbye to the body
flamed into a maddening nothing. You didn't even die—

was that the problem? Hardly to do with her
or with him. Sometimes I set aside the afternoon
to relive what feels like caricature: walks under
the George Washington Bridge, neither of us knowing

to enjoy the company. Time's passed, yes,
left me a diamond of bitterness. I see the water brace
itself for my reflection, circle the stitch where absence
dropped its anchor—but I'm alive and capable
of meditation. Walking through chokecherry trees,
language seems accomplice to grieving; everything
dissolves to make words possible. Joy sours,
brevity distends, silence tows its dragline to the finish.

Poem, close your palm: you ask nothing in return.
Think how far you've come through afternoons and evenings
when loss seemed to whistle from the manholes,
your hands staining everything with blackberry blood.

HUMMINGBIRD

Knocking against my southwest window,
I mount a feeder, inviting her vandalism.
And though a guest with too delicate a coat,
she never drops a feather, an unfulfilled parable,
while inside our losses gracelessly accrue
without logic or pattern, and we wonder at that:
what prepares a bird for so much failure
when all her body's work amounts to maintenance,
no spare change from a day's sugar water,
no breakthrough in song, no new nest.
My uncle dies on Christmas. My father
apologizes for crimes that went unnoticed
through fifty years of knowing. I've never
had a sibling, can't conceive of the collation,
but there are lessons I want to teach him
about birds, how they dare keep everything
precious in one place. The elastic safety
of the hummingbird's three eyelids
designed to protect her during flight.
She can close her lids and this spare space,
shut more light than a human eye, draw it
from a wound to guide the silence after.

WITTGENSTEIN IN THE PALISADES

The limits of my language are the limits of my world.

—Wittgenstein

The word *palisades* I've loved
as long as I can remember—

beginning in *palace*, ending in *aid*,
a word with no downside.

There I played foosball,
tended horses, held a hose,

waited to grow able-bodied
like the boys.

Say it wasn't where
my friend was killed

at fourteen, would my peripheries
slope differently?

In Manhattan, I watched
the seasons change

from a picture window
in a private library

and was blessed by the protection
of early life's omissions

when the families splintered
in my school and camp.

A skyline whose commuters saw
the mushroom cloud

on the GWB: I see
a forged memory.

*

I thought he must have died
that same year—

the events seemed
so cosmically similar—

but we shared the world
for two years

and never spoke of it.
(More things we never spoke of

than things we did.)
And when he died,

I thought I'd seen the worst
of what a person could do

without meaning to.

*

Though, sometime,
I must have fallen in love,

which took more room
than contemplating death,

and the slow, sad pleasure
of knowing it wouldn't last

more beautiful, even,
than imagining it would.

All of nature, ready
to encourage it: children's

silhouettes on paddleboards,
cicadas like prehistoric

hummingbirds, his fingers,
blistered, borrowed by the band.

Then autumn came:
the moment slipped between

the pages of death's folio.

*

September again,
the prohibitory blooms

never forget surface, and I'm
uncertain of their tact.

I have kept the body
I lived in then,

can't unhook the heft,
sirens like a pulse.

What promises to turn
into a kind of knowledge

continues·past catastrophe
to become accustomed.

A beautiful day: *severe clear*
the pilots called it.

They had to call it something.

*

It never goes away,
pulled by several moons,

this telegraphic
conversation with the past

for which there exists
no adequate word,

only addendums
based on the day.

How it changes with each
retired artifact or face,

one exaggerated palimpsest,
if, after all, you must

call everything something
or face a vast ineptitude.

*

And the later losses
inseparable from growth,

the ones that made me

limitless, his laughter
taking years to dry from my hair—

how, when I stole him back
from the years

through a broken fence
in memory,

neither of us could remember
what had made us glow

in the back seat—that ache
for what the years had kept

without my noticing,
their sleight of reasoning and hand.

THE COLOR WHEEL HAS BEEN CANCELED

Color spoils us, palette for each season; it's a shame for other, paler senses.
I can hardly smell an argument between two stars, what a murder the night
sky is behind clouds. Color echoes in every open eye, even when you'd like
to be unaccompanied. Wolves and birches in a tender binary. Only milk
and snow are truly white, the rest scurry from birth to blight on the color
wheel. Brides tarnish, calcium chips, the ermine only occasionally visits.
The diver can never unsee a coral, nor the lover the lover.

He gave me a moon garden, bouquet of truces on thin stems.
I was a hurricane, gutted and spun by my own hunger.
My mouth bred cavities, mouthfuls of argentine.

Never a sorer white than when I spoke. And spoken to,
I was a moon garden, earth and ether,
altered by my distances.

Sun fattens, bends over earth like a resistance band. Water glows, grows
frugal with moonlight. Manta rays glide like unfinished angels swallowing
a cameraman's spotlight.

EAGLE

Today's violence is cross-referenced
under technology.

An eagle shot in the face by a hunter
successfully receives

a replacement beak. I do not know
who these people are

who snipe the sky & walk off
when they know they've missed the heart.

I know the eyes that spot
the dying animal, abandoned

for what's called nature to deal with.
The hands responsible

for lifting the face & deciding to undo
what another human has done to it.

Someone will have to stabilize the bird
reading its deformity

for signs of infections.
Someone will have to see over

& over to suture the gash
where its beak once was,

·another, engineer the yellow arc
so the bird can be outfitted

with a second chance,
photographed for science, released back

into its world as if only just returning
from a day of hunting mice.

I wonder what the hunters think
of these efforts taken to undo

their recklessness, the delicate building
back to square one after a failed

annihilation, & whether the part
of the body that registers shame

is ever called upon to answer.

MEADOWLARKS AND MARKERS

In the woods of Arkansas where monster hog was shot, you guide a blind man up a tree. Explain the cones to me but explain them to me slowly: how a body develops between two markers, how the animals grow stranger, stronger each year.

With words, you draw a target on a blank canvas, talk of quiet places charged with wilderness. You, who hate the trigger's anthracitic smile. Who want to say *windlight* to the man and have it mean something.

Strange hallucinations: neon water in the river, cottonmouths rustling in shallow pits as couples exit the season's funny movie. Something lockjaws laughter. Something seen makes someone take a different path home.

Now get to the part where the hog walks onstage, its body fuller than the length between two cones—eight feet—and the blind man asks you if you've got one. You haven't got one, you say, just a set of meadowlarks, because a hog that size cannot be taken down.

Always, I imagine it is Milton asking, his dreams so vivid they burn through sight. Do you believe, like him, in the parable of talents, the entrusting and the multiplication? What tree bore the gun—who tends it? Not sacrifice, not pleasure. What am I asking you about terror? Your body lying the two of you to safety. Memory making more memory for me to write from. And why, when I think of you in this way, do I experience that panic of misplacing an answer in one's own mind, the poignant need to find it again, between miracles and omissions, meadowlarks and markers.

THE RETURN TO NATURE HAS BEEN CANCELED

I used to think, if things got bad enough,
I could return to nature, its bell-less door ajar.

But after living selfishly for so long, it was difficult
adjusting to a new set of house rules. The rain

outnumbered us, the snow's word was final,
and soon, nature grew tyrannical, tubercular magnolias,

extended lives of fruit flies. I missed the microwave's
electric coronas, draining a power bar to its last interval.

Men rushed to marry earthquakes. The frost
used my body as its workbench. Wind drew echoes

from every hunter's ear. *Come here*, the deer called
and speared them, getting even. I asked a historian

to peruse the index for what could happen next.
No one could focus on "the course of action,"

first a man with a megaphone, then a girl
with nothing but the wind tunnel of her palm.

SASHIMI

I served my loves' sashimi hearts
on iceless beds of clean bamboo.
Some were tasteless, others,
spoiled at the oil rig of our departure.
There was the horse mackerel
bucking at the rice, as if another life
were to await. The wheel shrimp
hugging his white station like a pillow,
the koi promising to love each grain.
I knew the knife work it had taken
to get here, the hands, my hands,
unfolding origami nerves, widening
fields between modest fish lungs.
I could smell blood on the stone floor,
heard a bell that signaled the start
of an auction. I plucked and plucked
at another urchin's stitches
as my own heart shivered on the scale.

WANDMAKER

Again I am thinking of the wandmaker,
his labor equal parts language and device,
whittling the wood, polishing a word.

How things must sometimes end up
in the wrong hands for history to happen.
Every bomb and every bomb maker

has a signature. Even the anchor
reading from a teleprompter
is surprised by what he has just had to say

and explains it's the particular bouquet
of shrapnel, breed of agony that marks
the maker. I try, but there's no way

to sleep off this violence. I spin in place
under a rainbow parachute pulled tight
by my kindergarten classmates.

Any one could be a runner in Boston.
The anchor reads the names of two
brothers, and I look for signs of certain

evil. Are these my people, my misguided
people, and how should I keep on
loving them, forgiving them; who can

teach you that, really? Everything
gets languaged eventually, even silence
flourishes rhetorically—*that's all for now*

folks, stay tuned. The wandmaker
tunes the wood then steps aside
for utterance to draw a sacrifice in air.

THE SEER DREAMS ANTIGONE

It is not advised to weep for the children of your enemies,
      though if you do it in the privacy
           of your home,   who can judge you?

And no one can tell you the order of action
is for the greater good
      if little seems in order, if even less
                    seems good.

            Oh, night is a compelling orator,
        the jasmines flicker on and off.

When your enemy sees your fig trees,
he will be reminded of his son's uneven hair,
      but in your brother he will find
only a poor imitation.

Do not let anyone catch you burying the body.

           Hide his body in your own
        until the lights go out,
then pray for negligence, black sails
      left unchanged,
           dull spot in the electric fence.

If you do not speak up for the body,
the wrong person will speak for it.

And who can say
if the mind is worse than what's out there
circling the night.

YOU ALWAYS WISHED THE ANIMALS
WOULD LEAVE

after the 2015 Tbilisi flood

Half the zoo mislaid, the reporter calls them *residents*, as though they lived in a gracious, gated community. Twelve Georgian men push one perplexed hippo: no Russell Crowe as Noah, no sidekick with a checklist. How to convince a lion to return to its cage when it's seen the Narikala lit at night? The things you wished would happen in this life have you caught in old affection, fresh confusion. In your version, the animals were never hungry or afraid. They climbed the trees of Tbilisi for a better view. The wolves returned to forests in the Trialeti Mountains. The fate of birds was ambiguous as the founding legend of King Gorgasali who, hunting, shot a pheasant that fell into a spring, cooked or healed, accounts differ. So the literal king named the place *Tpili* meaning "warm." Three brown bears lie limp in mud as police, in the ultimate video game sequence, big-game hunt the square at night. Your wish, succumbed to its alterations. At Mass, the priest reminds the congregation that bells and crosses melted down by communists became the bars of cages, the ticket operator's chair. You always wished the animals would leave, their problem-solving spirits put to use, lifting fruits from markets, befriending lonely citizens. But time twists your childhood dream until it's nothing but a game of telephone, just as the bird—or was it a deer, or the king himself—fell into the waters and was spared.

WE NEVER LIVED HERE

You visit: I start building a house I will have to burn down
when you leave.
                              Always July again
when it happens, month of purple rings around the moon

as we come up with ways to speak of winter, shovel love blues,
wet with wolfsnow.

The new you uses old you as leverage.

Again, I'm picking out Scandinavian lamps, and how
do we always end up here, with trappings no one can afford

and no floor to set them on?   You still see sadness on the side:

she makes you strap her in, makes you tell her off,
and maybe it's true I've never valued your love

or what it means for you to push her out of the way

to offer me a single lighthearted minute,
but can I still be the victim?
                              Where day ends, night volunteers,

and the switchback is infinite, harmless.

The living call this health—you didn't always have it,

and when I tried to buy it for you,
you wouldn't wear it out; when I poured it in a glass, for once,

you wouldn't drink.   July leaves me moonsick, laryngitic.

There's a door to enter desire and a door by which to exit.

Let's say it's a dog door and there's nothing to keep you
from coming and going as you please.

Ours is the empty room I can't vacate.   I polish the steel

fire escape hoping I can dupe a bird to scrapbook there.

It's obvious we never lived here:
ceiling stainless.   The impossible dustlessness.

THE SONG OF MALE AGGRESSION

Singing is one of the most common ways birds advertise that a territory belongs to them.

One boy offered me a necklace,
another cut it from my throat.
I'd forgotten until I heard the singing:
two robins in autumn disputing
open space. Once, I waited
without knowing for a nest
I could build in the dell of a voice.
Words for wanting bloomed in midair;
I learned to listen for variations.
What's not love in those words
finds others. But body, I was never
a bird leaving branches overhead
in case a dust hawk descends.
These men migrating from restlessness
to fatherhood, these birds perched
near the marrow of all memories
belong to me still, winding blue
through bowered nests. Sixteen,
we were always singing, were targets
ushered by longing and lament.
We split the silence and mended it.

AMERICAN COWBOY

When the politician takes
his gun out on stage,

we're meant to feel wonder
he hasn't shot us,

grateful to leave with our lives.

It nears the feeling, maybe,
in Plath's "Daddy,"

the boot in the face . . .

when the white man walks on stage
in cowboy boots and hat,

a shorthand.

But I don't wish his body
near my own—*hear it*—

don't mistake terror for adoration.

There's no plot in the Old Western,
only masculine delirium,

and the promise,
part childish, part challenge,

of frontier.

Gold humming in the nearest river.

Vigil of buffalo grazing though the night.

And the tumbleweed,
a complicated thing,

gaining momentum
around an emptiness.

Truly, inside is nothing,

and it protects that nothingness
that built it—

this, its language, its politic.

What will it take
to start over again

with a myth we might perhaps outlive?

It's the cowboy who the cowboy saves.

SECOND PASS

Months, I dream more *there* there. An evening in the old theater. A late-night drive for cigarettes. Something easily shared between strangers instead of warnings about diamondback snakes. Miles of corn in civilized formations. All the easily organic produce. All the equestrian Republicans. Slow circles on the Susquehanna one day, then the current racing itself.

Night brings a change in concentration. The stars are open for interpretation: kneecap or fin, dipper or spear. Often I dreamed the past in future presents, and in my dearest conjugational convictions, what was there seemed to withstand a change of tense.

But summer gives way to itself indefinitely, a stone skipped across its own plenitude. And now you are somewhere, doing something, under daylight. You are tired tonight and find rest. A great and gentle hand takes care of us. We find love, and even the failing is good. Even the itch of not finding and the absences are good, galaxies multiplying on the mind's surface.

And what might it feel like to say it plainly after so long spent finding an idiom? No one of you. No two. Ongoing. Never-love, now go. Be anywhere. Be somewhere.

PRIVATE CONSTELLATIONS

Every constellation begins in the mind.
Even its ascension is gentle, reasoned work.
Hard to distinguish bright from blight,
the mistreated wife, the wrongfully condemned
perched aside the hero and his hound.
A single thought takes light years to articulate,
settling on a shape like oil in water.
In this involute cartography, you get at night
what you put in daylight. A spatter of gossip
churns a minor galaxy while questions
recycled between philosophers and saints
pulsate through their destined paths
to moor at last in pensive sights. But the hands
that touched you before I had the chance
glow brightest in the galaxy tonight;
her fingers, wishbones in the shifting distance,
while below, cars bark like dogs I have
neglected, afternoon tarnishes like bronze.
Desires cross meridians to distinguish us.
The fickleness of stars shocks the native planets.

THE END OF THE WORLD HAS BEEN CANCELED

Pygmalion of anonymous days
glossed, fitted for the reckoning ball.

*

Dawn parts trawler fish,
lustrous deaths
on Seaport's docks.

*

What's the difference between
periphery & prophecy?

The end's a fence
deactivated at night.

*

I threaten the mailman with empty packages,
tell him I can smell greetings on his fingers,

the carmine ink & cadence of proposals
composed just under the wire.

*

What do we know of this tilting life,
fresh out of Babel & into outer space?

The fluency of arches, driftwood
of truces, light the rift between

tomorrow, no tomorrow,

two movies competing
for the same ticket.

KNOCKOUT MOUSE MODEL

A knockout mouse is a genetically engineered mouse in which researchers have inactivated, or "knocked out," an existing gene.

Its body and blood are teaching tools: islands of the genome's archipelago disabled, the conditioned chaos observed. Most won't grow past the embryo, designed for dissection, microscope eyes. A scientist spends his lunch hour contemplating the concealed sides of its origami heart.

How to say that suffering should yield something? How to say *trespass*, *hope*, *progress* stowed in the lax body, in one utterance?

Terror is imagining the human body intruded upon in this way, its furniture rearranged and forced to breed children. Someone coming in the night with helix scissors, clipping your eye color, turning off your hearing, switching out your liver for a third kidney, all of it happening slowly, like an old movie reel.

I feel my cells retreat into my fingers, ready to defend their information.

In a gentler, cartoonier universe, the mice would be anthropomorphically attractive: knockouts, mice who model. They'd drink on the house wherever they went, twirling their tails flirtatiously.

Tonight, the unstudied, parasitic mice are having the night of their lives, scaring couples on stoops, freeloading meals from granite floors. Deli cats hear them pacing behind walls. The excitement of their tiny footsteps is excruciating.

An off-duty scientist is breeding something for fun, to see what happens if—what happens? Nature's mice are breaking and entering, slipping under doors with all they need to survive.

LATE UNDER OCTOBER'S SUPERMOON

A gentle inequity among the elements
for it is water moonlight wants most,

her attention, unsuited for the human scope.
In the great rivers, bodies dissolve

per their remembered shapes. We wait
in October's din, concussive music,

and it is clear why we must sometimes
change our lives, for beauty or disfigurement.

The supermoon blooms a tyranny of flowers,
white-knuckled, milky as the Pear soap

that could not save the mild Victorians.
Here, amid the cradled objects,

I hear the tacit accusation in her light.
It's what we are that keeps a blight upon us.

BROKEN PERIODIC

No one who has ever had a childhood
wants what's happening. No one
who has ever wondered anything:
where the rain's headed in her steel hooves.
Questions wrongly put swell
like moths under a light. On the streets,
everything looks human. You forget
certain animals are bloodless injured.
You must imagine some other color
that means hurt. At night, you sleep
with something like your gifts: to anguish
and ascribe a language, music.
To slice a fig the long way and linger.
To grieve for a country.
To grieve without a country to grieve.

TERRIBILITÀ

I don't want to die in a European city,
shoved off a bridge into a river,
the police never finding where I've gone.

I don't want to die in a crowded museum
home to your favorite triptych or statue,
survey the lone van anywhere I cross.

The Old Masters I studied in AP—
each century, someone intending
beauty for the others. Weak-kneed

for the boys of Caravaggio, I wasn't afraid
of what the world might do to me,
trusted desire leaves us hurt but whole.

This, my education. A kind of petition.
I trim stems on the diagonal. Burn threads.
Oil wood. From this neurotic utility

blooms a way forward. I write you
so you know I'm not dead in Brussels
or London or Toulouse. I used to think

beauty the point, or one of them.
Those places where even the spaces
unintended for admiration offer a reprieve.

And look, how the people are lifted
from their lives without human signature
or grace. What is this world we are making

for each other? A slaughter that cannot
be rendered or mean. Who will study it
from the back of the darkened class,

by the silence of the projector's click.

AMERICAN FAITH

In Buddhism, difficult people are thought to be a gift.
This explains why I'm not a Buddhist.
I love the glib, slick farce of hardheartedness,
though I've held my human head
in my human hands so it would not
succumb to language. It was earth that taught me
names for all the planets, how to look
at an angle for the hummingbird,
dark satellite of sugar in the blossom's mouth.
I could picture that vast absence of us,
moons spinning coolly in unscripted pasts.
But when I try to imagine our president,
understanding imagination is the basis
of all faith, I suffocate on hatred's loneliness.
I can't stand the unity of my own hands,
how no part leads the writing of a word.
But this, too, is no faith that can be held,
scalds without tributary purpose. Like something
held to the light by its edges, I see the long years
ahead of me, full of voices of friends'
children's children. I want a kind of betterness.
Want it desperately. Is that faith? While the days,
impatient, fresh beasts, appeal to me—
You are here now. You must believe in something.

PALIMPSEST

Flower-bordered river
where I fillet the hyacinths,

a Russian doll of places
posing as one place.

Halogen me
at a horse show in Florida

while another juliennes
olives for appetizers.

A doll slipped in another
till all dolls are dull:

versions of me
with whistles for lips

reciting asterisks
in the periodic table.

Collage of the unconscious:
white flowers, lost teeth,

scarecrow with
an aureole of straw,

basilica for everyone's
best dresses.

I visit the public
museum of clouds,

lithographs of sky
posing as space.

Layers make monsters
as shows the snapdragon.

Memory, you crooked thing
I do to the page.

A TECHNIQUE FOR OPERATING
ON THE PAST

My great-grandfather held a brain and studied it for signs of music.
Like all the men in my family, he was a close reader and musician.

The day the KGB arrived to take him, his students misplaced
the combination to the ether closet. I see him in the armamentarium

choosing between scalpels and scopes, escaping across
the Carpathians in peasant clothes. True, he did not love the state,

a symphony full of poorly written solos. But he could hold a brain
more steady than any in the university, interrogate its perilous

longitudes, cardinal directions for taste and melancholy, yellow tulips,
joy. I see him peeling back the hair, that quiet, necessary artifice,

to reveal a nesting doll of impulses, then reciting the cold, hard rain
of these connections at conferences in Cambridge. A halo of stage

whispers as he came as close to candor with the mind as was possible.
He understood the officer's parietal lobe where his punishment

waited to be articulated, its obstinacy illustrated in early phrenology
by the silhouette of a ram. Always the doctor's burden to reason

with that which cannot easily be reasoned. I see him make the first
incision, certain, gentle as a breaststroke in the Black Sea. He knew

how to tell the brain a story, listen when told one in return. Knew
that engine of ephemera could be a sentencing, a silence or a song.

ACKNOWLEDGMENTS

I am grateful to the editors of the following publications in which versions of these poems first appeared:

Colorado Review, Day One, DIAGRAM, Fence, Field, Kenyon Review, The Literary Review, Los Angeles Review, The Moth, Narrative, The Paris-American, Poetry London, PN Review, Prelude, Southword, and *Tin House*.

"Broken Periodic" was published as part of the 92Y's #ANewColossus.

"A Technique for Operating on the Past" appeared in the *2015 Hippocrates Prize Anthology* (edited by M. W. Hulse and D. R. J. Singer, Hippocrates Press, 2015), and later appeared in the *British Journal of Psychiatry* (June, 2016).

"A Technique for Operating on the Past" won first place in the Hippocrates Prize for Poetry and Medicine.

"Hummingbird" won first place in the Gregory O'Donoghue International Poetry Prize, and "Sashimi" won third.

"We Never Lived Here" was the recipient of the Martin Starkie Prize from the Oxford Poetry Society.

"Yard Sale," "The Master's Pieces," "The Return to Nature Has Been Canceled," won second place in the Narrative Annual Poetry Contest.

"Uranium in English" won the *Event Horizon* magazine competition.

"You Always Wished the Animals Would Leave," won second place in the Magma Poetry Competition.

NOTES

"Uranium in English"
Uranium was discovered by Martin Heinrich Klaproth, a German chemist, in the mineral pitchblende (primarily a mix of uranium oxides) in 1789. Uranium glass (glass to which uranium has been added, resulting in a green glow) is sometimes known as Vaseline glass for its greasy appearance.

"The Bees Have Been Canceled"
For Virgil on the subject of bees, see *The Georgics*.

"Meditation Having Felt and Forgotten"
This poem owes its opening phrase to "Meditation at Lagunitas" by Robert Hass.

"Eagle"
Volunteers at the nonprofit group Birds of Prey Northwest were instrumental in nursing Beauty, a bald eagle shot in the face sometime in 2005, back to health. A raptor specialist and a mechanical engineer later teamed up with scientists, even a dentist, to design a nylon polymer beak replacement for Beauty.

"Meadowlarks and Markers"
This poem is for Joshua Manuel. In the Parable of Talents (Matthew 25:14-30), a master entrusts three servants with his money, gold and silver talents while away. The first two servants use their talents, thus multiplying them, and presumably earning a profit for the master. The last servant plays it

safe and does not use his talent, choosing to bury or hide it. This servant is seen as faithless in the eyes of the Lord.

"You Always Wished the Animals Would Leave"
The flooding of the Vere River valley in Tbilisi, the capital of Georgia, on the night of June 13, 2015, resulted in the death of at least twenty people. The Tbilisi Zoo lost half of its animals; while the majority were killed by flooding, many escaped their cages, roaming freely through Tbilisi before they were rounded up over subsequent days.

"We Never Lived Here"
I owe *wolfsnow* to "The Loss of the *Eurydice*" by Gerard Manley Hopkins: "Hailropes hustle and grind their / Heavengravel? Wolfsnow, worlds of it, wind there?"

"Late under October's Supermoon"
Three supermoons preceded and followed the 2016 election: October 16, November 14, and December 14. British Pears soap advertisements are an example of egregious racism in the marketing of nineteenth-century goods.

"Terribilità"
This poem is for John Loughery.

"A Technique for Operating on the Past"
This poem is dedicated to my great-grandfather, Grigore T. Popa, a remarkable doctor, scholar, and activist.

THANK-YOUS

Part of what motivates writers through years of submissions and revisions is the earnest hope of one day writing such a page.

Thank you to John Loughery, whose keen critical eye is unmatched, and whose friendship is one of the greatest joys in my life.

To all the non-writer friends who faithfully support their writer friends, especially Kelly Rodigas, Emily Dunn, Michael Dean, Meredith Grossman, and Emma Mortensen.

To poets Jen Levitt, Lizzie Harris, Jenny Xie, Nicole Sealey, Ben Purkert, Daniel Martini, Jane Draycott, Jamie McKendrick, Eduardo Corral, Ricardo Maldonado, Caroline Bird, Tracy Brimhall, Averill Curdy, Meghan O'Rourke, Catherine Barnett, and every person who helped make these poems better, and whose own writing brings beauty into the world.

Thank you to all of my graduate professors at NYU and Oxford University; in particular, to Deborah Landau, who helped shape this book, and Jenny Lewis, whose support and friendship spans the Atlantic.

To Barnard College; Saskia Hamilton for her insight and patience; Mary Gordon, for her wisdom and depth; and Debora Spar, for her fearless example.

To the English Department at the Nightingale-Bamford School; especially fellow writers Laura Kirk, Betsey Osborne, and Brad Whitehurst. And to Christine Schutt, who so wisely and generously nurtured my love of writing.

Thank you to Brenda Shaughnessy and Craig Morgan Teicher whose individual and collective gifts have inspired and guided me for the last decade.

To *Poetry*, *Publishers Weekly*, *Poets & Writers* Magazine, the Munster Literary Centre, and the 92Y for their mentorship and support, and for all they do to nurture communities of writers.

To my family, today and every day.

Finally, to my husband, Sam Nester, for the last eight years of laughter and inspiration, and our dog, Chaucer, for the last four years of early morning wake-ups.

MAYA C. POPA is the Poetry Reviews Editor at *Publishers Weekly* and an English teacher and director of the Creative Writing Program at the Nightingale-Bamford school in NYC. She is the recipient of The Poetry Foundation's Editor's Prize, and her poetry appears in *Tin House, Kenyon Review, The New Republic*, and elsewhere. Her criticism and non-fiction appear widely, including in *Poetry, The Times Literary Supplement, Poets & Writers* Magazine, and *The Huffington Post*. She holds degrees from Oxford University, NYU, and Barnard College.

SARABANDE BOOKS is a nonprofit literary press located in Louisville, KY. Founded in 1994 to champion poetry, short fiction, and essay, we are committed to creating lasting editions that honor exceptional writing. For more information, please visit sarabandebooks.org.